A Hunch about Water

poems by

Morgan D. Bazilian

Finishing Line Press
Georgetown, Kentucky

A Hunch about Water

For my parents who always encouraged me to write

and

Cian and Debbie—for everything else

Copyright © 2025 by Morgan D. Bazilian
ISBN 979-8-89990-081-5 First Edition
All rights reserved under International and Pan-American Copyright Conventions. No part of this book may be reproduced in any manner whatsoever without written permission from the publisher, except in the case of brief quotations embodied in critical articles and reviews.

Publisher: Leah Huete de Maines
Editor: Christen Kincaid
Cover Art: Bob Ryan, *Solstice*
Author Photo: Whit Richardson
Cover Design: Elizabeth Maines McCleavy

Order online: www.finishinglinepress.com
also available on amazon.com

Author inquiries and mail orders:
Finishing Line Press
PO Box 1626
Georgetown, Kentucky 40324
USA

Contents

I. So Long since I've Seen the Ocean

Children 1
War 2
The Seaside 3
Water on land 4
Dublin 6
Morning 7
My little boy is sitting on flowers 8
Barely talking 9
The Drunk 10
Birds 11
Breathing 12
Statistics 13
Equations 14
The guru 15
Evening 16
He says 17
Photographs 18
Rolling 19
Then time 20
Conjuring 21
Peat 22
Harbinger 23
Acquisition 24
Chords 25
Puddles 27
Coda 28
Shared 29

II. I know I am Like the Rain

Love goes downhill 33
My Little Boy Asks 34
Commuting 35
Screens 36
Flies 37
Sunrise 38
Window 39
Faith 41
Next to me 42
The Plane 43
Skype 44
Arriving 45
Hurry and wait 46
Liver 47
Bedtime 48
Typical 49
Voicemail 50
So much softer than I did back then 51

Dedicated to Professor Alan B. Howes, a former editor of the Norton Anthology of Poetry, who reminded me that, "a panther pisses where he pleases."

I. So Long since I've Seen the Ocean

Children

The girls watch him
Run around him
See his hair move
(Wispy on the top like a cloud).

He is smiling at them
Picking them up, making faces
He is falling asleep while they yell,
Climb over him.

They witness time,
Unaccompanied or directed,
Unaware of gravity
Or its incongruity.

They cannot help skipping
Laughing, forgetting.
Inadvertently inventing space
Dimensions and worlds.

The little girl screams for help
Happily secured
In the branches of a small tree;
A kingdom in the sky.

She forgets,
Looks around accusingly,
And then yells again
To no one in particular.

She becomes distracted
New buds touch her cheek,
Retreating into full leaves,
And a caterpillar without wings.

Her age
Entirely
Defying
Gravity.

War

A memory unfading,
After years of deliberation
Détente, liberation,
After years of quiet.

The mortar awakened,
To remind the young,
To ensure a lineage,
A transition to history.

The sound still shocking
Forty years from fear,
Continents and presidents removed
From burned monasteries.

The pine forest now still
The floor not soft enough
To dampen the impact
Or remove the smell.

Words leaving echoes.
They are dancing now,
Separating.

Becoming letter and notes,
Derived from copper strings
Reverberating against wood.

The dictionary avoided, mistrusted
Returning to fragments
To families placed on paper

A song not sung
A book unwritten
The effect forgotten.

The Seaside

Houses growing from the bay.
Black rock creeping from the sand.
The water reaching for the road.

The town nearly quiet.
A young girl driving too fast
Down small roads.

An old harbour
Facing an older church
Reachable only at low tide.

The beach faces North.
The boats are man made,
Wood stretched over angled hulls

The fishing is good
For salmon and gar.
The sea transparent.

Two small pubs
Their taps run late
Acting as modern lighthouses.

An evening coming swiftly,
Composed of a girl
And a vivid memory.

A scent of sandalwood
Infused into the fabric,
The center of the world.

A change of name
A brown, seaweed-smelly landscape,
A pool of clarity.

Warmer than the big sea
Protected by mussels,
Clams, sharp stones, and a promise.

Water on land

A small road to the sea
Grass growing in between tire treads
Sand invading its edges
Small brown caterpillars mark the end.

The rising of dunes
Deep trails up false ridges
Through tall grasses
Nearly coordinated in movement.

Wind blowing directly on-shore
The waves unorganized
Cracked rocks covered in orange moss
The sky coloured deeply with reflection.

My hands tucked-in deeply
Shoulders slightly raised
Eyes blinking quickly
And a long exhale.

The water's pronounced movement
Uneven;
Standing and breaking

The flags flapping, making noise
Indicating direction,
Vying for attention.

The white froth
Blown backward to sea,
Reflecting light
Creating a near inverse of a sine.

A plane so thin
Short lived, transparent
And completely quiet.

And then a break, a thump,
And a decision.
Even with the wind's support
The wave unable to meet the land.

Dublin

Dublin in the sun
Stilted and foreign
Not used to the attention

The light moving into the corners and cracks
The bits of dust
The drunks, pale skin turned red

She showed herself
Down Camden Street
With the flowers and the fruit from Spain

The people squint from inside pubs
Or out on the quay drinking light pints
The canal starting to smell

Old men rolling up their pants
In Stephen's Park
Winding trails of asphalt

Thrown out fried food
Mixed with glass
And dried blood on the curb

Then the night
A small red tinge in amorphous clouds
And a hint of quiet

Morning

I can see it in my head
The small wisps
Forced off the windswept ridge in unison

Yet they cling
And now they go to the sky together
Like a veil amongst things not as fragile

The light comes softly in quietly
Waking up in the mountain air
The sun does not exaggerate herself

The first breath of the day sits low in the valleys
Conforming to indentations and filling in gaps
Before being dissipated

Your eyes look up

The small hydrogen atoms forming
To make something more than themselves
The release is just phenomenal

Imagine the mathematics

My little boy is sitting on flowers

My little boy is sitting on flowers.
The flowers are made of light.
They look like daisies.
He is watching them move across the floor and smiling at them, then at me.
It is beautiful to watch, and yet I feel sick.

He smiles again at me, then them,
Then a little boy handing him a car.
He rolls it across the lighted floor
And the daisies move with him.
Like magic.

I feel like I can't stand up.
That I can't move at all.
But I have to keep watching him, and them.
If I lose sight of him, even for a moment,
My stomach sinks
And I get incredibly scared.

My chest tightens.
But he is right there,
The lights in the floor now look like cars
He is in awe.
Like magic.

The shrink's words are the only ones I can access.
Like I am holding up a ball.
The ball is like a bubble,
Not like the concrete I used to carry in my childhood dreams.
It is fragile and dented and slippery.
Then it turns to glass,
And I am losing my grip.

Barely talking

Their movements are hushed
Quick smiles fade
Rhythms un-syncopated
Hesitated and dense.

Staring at the Thinker
Green trees, old and well maintained
Rocks and trails, benches of iron,
Words spoken slowly, quietly.

Sitting close but not touching
Looking out
With Air-dried tears
A living statue.

A moment forgotten
And then repeated.
Sadness reflected
Embedded in copper and iron.

Yelling aside, he is quiet.
Snow drifting like moving silence
Half way up the door
To the corners of the windows.

The subdued smell of huskies.
Another day of even light
Tempered by the fjord, the haze
And the diesel.

He inhales nothing but smoke.
Still silent,
Living with regret,
He fumes.

The Drunk

A room
Without echoes
Painted the colour of sky
Masquerading as nature.

Enclosed
In a cell
Made solely of salted sticks,
And bourbon.

Without cause, he reacts
The drunk. Fighting with air
Pushing his arms,
Moving his lips.

The stubble on his face
Raised above the dry peeling skin
His neck vein bulged.

Knocking down things in his path:
Family, friends,
Old boxes, rotted vegetables.

His conviction without bounds
Or reason or focus.
Eventually forgetting,

Falling asleep over a heater;
Exhaust fumes creating vivid dreams
Of a life.

Birds

The cloud created by a brush stroke
The paint slow to dry
A day's end

And the three birds
Return to me again

Only in the cold,
At dusk, over a forest,
Near the sea and glaciers,

Alpenglow
In the far north

Taking off from the pine trees
To show me the west
And reflections from their wings

Some short calls
That do not translate
(understood in part)

I welcome their return
Transfixed
Humbled

Forgetting (almost)
What they tell me
Each time

Reminded again:
There are uncountable places
Our telescopes cannot yet see

Breathing

Now he is sitting
(maybe lying) in the bed
A white room
Too small

He has grown thin and pale
The smile is forced just a bit
The confidence stripped bare
By the brutality of the light

And lungs that fail
Coughed a hole in one
And they do not heal

Hard to see him bow down
And catch his breath
Wheeze and spit
And swallow and try to laugh

But he is just reminding the rest of us
Of our time
And meat and bones
And fluids

Statistics

A statistician without recourse to the sky,
An esoteric problem defined.
Simplified and abstracted
Beyond recognition,
Beyond integrity.

Memories tied together,
Strung up like a clothesline.
Wooden and plastic clips belie their strength.
Supporting immense weights
Of symbols and paradigm.

Remembering an old teacher,
And advice well given.
Instruction on rebellion
And long days without resolve
Wasting time, as if it mattered.

Equations

A dazzling array of pedagogy
An astounding inventory of facts
Arranged as neat and linear
Rows of algebra, of symbols.

Trying to explain in a hurry
Events that required millions of years
Outside the boundary of vocabulary,
Now dormant.

An altogether awesome attempt
At explanation
Entirely misguided,
Yet not small minded.

A latte on the street.
Cream spilling over the sides.
Brushed by walkers, workers, strollers,
And children's hands.

A bright sun tempered
By winter and its distance.
Worlds passing by.
A piece of significance or philosophical infamy,

Bamboo chairs and forgetfulness.
A scene captured only on paper
Partially drawn in perspective,
Two-dimensional, but real.

The guru

The guru of what?
Of love
of space, death, dirt

And whatever there is to be heard or seen
can be done through
a haze or a small hole or lace

The log has fire
inside it
holding back

God inside a costume
reprimanding the rest of us
searing our breath.

A letter (one of many)
a note
music in the air

They were meant to be songs
just verse now
plain on the paper and without texture

Old coals white
still some not fully burnt
the night as memory

I hope you (she) can hear me
through the rain
and time zones

Although distant,
words altered and jumbled,
still comprehensible

The humanity apparent in every parentheses
The melancholy in the passive voice

Evening

It goes down slowly
slower than believed
or modeled, or assumed

It goes down with a slight guitar riff
a finger picking rhythm
in standard tuning

Drunken and swaying
he dances
sailing through the night

The paleness of the girl
and the moon
at the same time

Forgetting the difference
her dress beautiful and delicate
torn at the neck her hair tumbles

The burden is now on the evening
and its possibilities

No matter where you go
some small bit of you
some small song

It is wholly unnecessary
to explain this to anyone
but ourselves

The rest of the place is (nearly) silent

He says

He says he is settled

A new baby
making faces
and little noises

An old house
a porch, a scent of smoke
of willow

And driving home
without traffic
he notices that he has turned old

There is distance and trepidation
Days flitted away that years ago
would have counted for very little

Now precious
and well thought out
Planned, pruned

It takes hours to forget the noise
the repetition
The undo button useless here

Photographs

Pictures bent on the mantle
held up by other things:
books, boxes, a vase

The people smiling, moving
hands splayed, touching
They look straight ahead

And by now they have forgotten where he went
when he left
a journey not yet complete

Another frame shows a moment:

The sun low, late autumn
arms intertwined
posed and casual

A small wisp of light
remains in the depression of a cliff

The three women are smiling
and young
each looking in different directions at different cameras

Today they rarely speak
attentions diverted
dusted only rarely

Rolling

The clouds rolling,
shifting, showing gray underbellies
insides full of particles

Breathing in and out
the cycle apparent from the porch
agonizing in its apparent slowness

The temperature gradient, land and sea
Providing a lovely dichotomy
A light drop of rain in the middle of an altogether sunny day

The side of the tree that faced the wind
standing now shaven
brutally cold but unyielding

Hours pass
the sun identifies
the imperfection in the grain

And now a question about the sun itself
as we pencil in some of the dimensions of the world
into its skin

Searching for size and geometry in a storm

Then, time

His daughter sighs
And he forgets days and years.

She breathes quickly
A small noise like a whisper,
Like she is talking.

Moving her hands, her legs
Like a snow angel.

Lips mimicking sound
Eyes rolling under closed lids
He cannot stop watching.

She wakes in starts and fits
Grabbing his finger as an anchor.

The washing machine as background noise,
as soundtrack,
to new lives.

Then, time…

Exaggerated family bonds,
Attempts at reconciliation
Gracefully retracted.

Emancipation and a feeling of guilt.
A long drive through a familiar desert,
And another encounter.

Distance interpreted through a baseball cap,
The un-confidence of blue eyes,
Hugs instead of kisses.

Forgotten affection,
Tradition, and ceremony.
People separated by plane rides.

Conjuring

Not even the matriarchal nature of a bluebird
Goes unnoticed

In a day stilted towards evening,
Leaning towards hope

The bird watchers witnessing ceremony,
Impervious to suggestion or iteration

The slightest whisper of the trees
Informing their perspective of the world

Reformed in an instant
Of echoes and negative space

Their blindness without border
Conjuring only emptiness

The sunlight evasive,
Yet intent on bearing weight

My mind disassembling memory
Holding onto things not appropriate

A vision of the future in overalls,
A mindset of luminous perfection

Creating a frightening present
Uninspired, thin, nervous, and antiquated

The imagination of a beggar
Looking at a life nearly half over

An inference about the solubility of dreams,
The placement of hardening resolve

About tomorrow
And the day after

Peat

The peat recently revealed to the sun
Cut and drying
Exposed on the sides

The sheep creating dust from water.
A floating lake
Above old weakened stone

The bog captures my shoe
Its softness
A partial solution for old knees

A hill steeped with yellow flowers
And heather
And autumn

Detail and color
A landscape of low skies and gray
Immersion and resistance

Planted regret
Diffused doubt

Dreams infused with age
Frayed and rusting

Children with no memory
Unable to cite person, place or date.

Mediated ideals
Negotiated interests

Small contributions
Amounting to copacetic smiles

The day wholly unimpressed
By the human condition

Harbinger

Recurring thoughts
Like old day dreams

Virtual reality
Occurring at the margins of sleep

A vision of something,
Someone, which cannot be verbalized

A picture of a place, an association,
A moment not available

Love as a symbol of identity,
Love as the harbinger of the world

The generalizations of memory
Like smoothed functions
And a slight pang of loss

The years diluted
Colors forgotten
Vocabularies dulled

Closing my eyes
I cannot define the scenes,
Only small bits without clues

Time moving wildly
Without even a hint of sarcasm
(As if in the middle of a joke)

Acquisition

The world made smaller
By time, acquisition, paychecks
The weight of acceptance.

Acquiescence without analysis
Logic used without restraint
Tolerance allowed too often.

More ordinary than expected
Day dreams of change
Real dreams unrecalled.

The simple spinning
Producing nostalgia
An easy path to regret.

On an otherwise somnolent evening:

The same fear I saw years ago
The laugh tainted slightly
Shaking hands and bravado.

A propensity for images
As allegory
And then belief.

The eyes dampen
Laughter falls from the lips
The darkness replaced by pills.

Directed by denial and religion
(utterly wasteful
and petrifying to witness).

Chords

Inventing a song with no firm utterance.
Words displaced among images flying.
Chord shapes renamed to suit a style.

It goes on and grows,
Higher frets
And accompaniment.

Opportunities for intuition,
Formed as solos
Rhythms on the pick guard.

They are communicating
Through cameras,
Through semi-closed eyes.

Feeling the other in off-beats,
In innuendo,
In conjecture of elbows.

Retreating out of sight
The pair join palms.
The stage lights mimic emotion.

Languages intertwine
With gestures like branches
People speak slowly.

Pointing
Hesitant
Spreading their arms.

The dialogue stutters
Interrupted
Stochastic.

The words creating alternatives
Other scenes
A story unending.

Meandering
Repeating itself
And un-translated.

Puddles

Silence
in my head
pondering decisions
stumbling onto faults

Areas of slow growth
or fragile moss
(alive for decades or centuries
or minutes)

Clearing away
brown and green memories
revealing hard stone
unassailable and alive

We all carry these boulders
some are just less camouflaged
and now in a place carved out of forest
and sand and dirt; mangoes and palms

Claiming a life
on a road made of puddles and rock

It is a gentle sound I hear
and then again like a heartbeat
a snare drum or a rhythm
rain and wind

And then it is gone
moving over the small lake
its reeds and bogs
and evaporating

Aging upwards
to be caught in the atmosphere
deposited in a new place
without memory

Coda

It is like a coda,
a repeating section of a life
a day revealing itself
to a child

A tiresome parade of fears
guilt
pride
god

Discoveries of the mind
reflected (nearly identically)
in stories from another century
or just a myth

Not following,
but mooing
without decay
or fragility

A space beyond moisture
cracked, parched
it is beyond touch
nothing can adhere to its surface

A topsy-turvy space
unable to reflect
unable to store energy
and yet continually

Returning

Shared

It is not easy
not after years
not after days of laughing
days of fear
or sleep or sex

Different perceptions
of space,
varying illusions,
references,
definitions of words

A universe unique,
seen only from one set of eyes
bounded,
parochial,
and not entirely shared

She flows and tumbles
like a creek
loud and then hushed
sparkling at some angles
small eddies holding old feelings

She floats downstream
feet first
caught by old sticks
or rocks
too tired to move

Despite this
she and the waves
remain standing
immobile
against the rains

II. I know I am Like the Rain

Love goes downhill

He runs
And I alight
The corner of his mouth turns serious
And I laugh

The clichés used as a foundation
Building a perspective
Of how a child grows
More quickly than expected, etc.

My father calls
Expecting something
Not unreasonable things
Thanks or devotion

And I realise:
Love goes downhill
Towards the child
As sure as gravity

Like any other river
Or material flow
Or quantum of energy or heat
It takes the easiest path

My Little Boy Asks

My little boy asks,
"Is it tomorrow yet?"

I tell him,
"Not yet. Almost"

He nods,
But unsure.

Then, moving on
to trucks, trains, dinosaurs.

Making "vroom, vroom" noises,
Like boys do.

Then "grrrrr" noises
And those make me laugh.

I try to watch
His face

He rubs
The back of his hand on my arm

Up and down
Like a paintbrush

Like an elephant trunk
Wrapped around a leg.

I am lost again
Forgetting to pay attention

Making too many links
Analogies, similes

I am snapped back
By his feet

One, slightly turned inward
Just like mine.

Commuting

A day breaks
Unfettered by guilt
or gravity. The foothills
seem to be laying back,
as if reclining. The dirt
sighs, aware of the heat that will
return unabated. The water flattens
and seems to shutter in the face of the first light.
Receiving all kinds of waves, long and short,
and some that go right through it. I am
slowly putting on a shirt in the guest
room. Quietly moving to the door,
car, airport. So early that the
suburban sprinklers are just
starting their pre-programmed
cycles. And I can't tell if it is
morning or night.
The sky providing
No answers.

Screens

A hero, a scourge
        Detritus, detrimental
                Elegiac

All piling up in my head
        And the small room explodes
                Or seems to

And my boy is crying
        On the screen
                A bad dream

About trees and
        Not being able to see me
                I look down

At the carpet
        A colour I cannot place
                Furniture that is old

And dented
        And scratched
                And imprinted upon

With my fist and then fingers
        And then head
                I turn the phone away from me

So he does
        not see
                my tears

Flies

The river was much bigger
than I expected,
wider
darker.

The walk was more difficult
than I had hoped
uneven
loose dirt.

The fish were closer to
the rocks,
so my line
was short.

The boys on the other side
looked bored
and superior
almost sleepy.

It got dark
quickly.
The trail fading
into the river

and the road.
The edges
disappearing
entirely.

Sunrise

Not another poem
About the sunrise
The car seems to bend
Towards the colours
Rising

The people used to it
Have been awake for hours
Irrigating fields
With metal monsters

The fields not touched
Are already brown
Or fallow

Grain silos without
Shadows are the darkest
And coolest objects on the plains

The large pick-up trucks
Are dominating the roads
They appear proud
In the dark light

It cannot be ignored
The clouds are no longer hesitant
But in rapture
And the shades of orange and yellow
Swirling headstrong among the blue

Window

He is sitting
As if waiting

Wanting and then
Not

His back slides
Further

Hands on the buzzing
Keyboard

Humming from the street
Below

And then a crack
A wince

And his hands shake and
Eyes water

He looks at the image
Of his boy

On a bike
With a dog

In autumn colours
His face turned

And he is weeping
And exploding

And muttering
And pounding

And then nothing
Back to the keyboard

The whizz of the cars
Muted through the office window

That will not open

Faith

The images of school children
Dead and
Arms up
Like they are resting
Stars
Are everywhere
And the wreckage of a
Great plane

With burning rubble
And skin
And I am now weakened
And dulled
So that I do not
Feel a thing
At the site of this
Carnage

Focusing instead
On my performance
Metrics
And rhythms of
Holiday planning
And school breaks
And oil changes
"Nothing new

To look at
Here"
Scream the media
And so I obey
And turn my head
Down
To focus on lines
In the pavement

Next to me

This time my boy is next to me
sitting with the arm rest up.
My hands on his feet
he is deciding what the clouds look like
how he can feel the engines in his stomach
how he misses his momma.
This time his feet move
against my leg
his hand keeps raising the window shade
looking at the circles and squares
of green and brown
the very straight lines in between them.
The plane hums and rolls
oblivious to the fact
that my son is here
and my eyes are dry.
This mundane,
simplicity
is earth shattering
to almost no one
        but me.

The Plane

It is
Meant
To look like
A modest
Plane. But
One whose wings
Are not entirely real, but
Are made from smoke and magic and stardust and sunblasts.
A plane so fast that it blurs physics, imagination, sight, love, and form.
In its cargo
Is everything
Hope
Hate
Presence
Futility
Dharma
Skin
Bones
Colour
And
A
Small
Insistence
Of
Reality.

Skype

The image seems too small
My son only appears in the corner
He is moving quickly
as usual
Trying to show me something
Dada dada
and opening his eyes wide
and whispering loudly
and tilting his head
It is a toy jet I think
or maybe a Transformer car
or just a coloured pencil
I can't tell
The connection goes blurry a bit
but I don't want to stop his flow
Then he wants to say goodbye
and is told to say "I love you dada"
So he does
Twice and then again
And he is looking for the red button
and laughing and moving
and he finds it
and everything is too quiet

Arriving

On another night somnolent
After a sandwich
Wet from sitting in the bag
The promise of orange still in the sky

The cloud base tattered
And weathered
And broken and whole
Wisps and hints and sparks

The flight delayed two hours
A crazy woman in the front seat
An angry naval officer in tan
In a middle seat

Grown men doodling
Talking of their frequent flyer levels
Doing those ridiculous numbers games
That are three by three

The parking lot is quiet
The hood of my car pock-marked
From a long-gone hail storm
The sky almost clear

Forty-year-old songs on the radio on the drive home
The automatic pilot of a toll road
The heavy lights of a new gas pad
My little boy nearly magic on arrival

Hurry and wait

Men in double-pleated pants
Tan, with cuffs
Walking everywhere
With the cell phones on their hips
In little black holders that make a "flip" sound
Some with blue-tooth devices attached in their ears
Some watching old football games on tablets.

Other folding slices of pizza and eating
Their eyes wild and hungry
Napkins scrunched up in their right hands
The slices in their left
Trying to get it all done while
Faking to pay attention
To their colleagues
Cheap fake leather computer bags
with too many zippers
big metal watches with lots of pockets.

And then a small twinkle or spark or humanity
in their eyes
as they mutter at the pilot
to get the plane
the fuck off the ground
so they can get home in time
to put their kids to bed.

Liver

I try to yell at him
In my head
Dawn is near
Open your eyes
(The blue eyes of a baby
Even as a man)
And see it
But he ignores me

In a coma
Six years old
When he wakes
He has lost himself
Somehow
Like he is always out of breath
But won't open his mouth
He moves in to the top floor

Of an old mansion
Somewhere in Minnesota
And I don't hear from him again
For years
Then one day on the phone
Madness in his lilt
Madness in his stutter
And I cringe at the sound of it

I remember his father
Sanding the floors
Of our college shared house
Firm grip, strong hands
Hair parted and fading
And today a text
A kidney failure
And my big, strong friend
Is dead

Bedtime

Their boy is sweet
He has a sweet smile
His eyes downturned
His hands always in a light fist

He was smiling a lot
And moving his feet
They turn inward
The toes wiggling at each other

He finds that funny
And stares
And then remembers
We are there visiting him

He has on pile bedclothes
With sports balls on them
Baseballs and basketballs
Footballs and drool

He doesn't get up
When we arrive
He sits and waits and yells for us
To see him

He tells us that his bus is coming
He takes it to special school
Each day
He doesn't want to sleep

His mother smiles at him
Holds his hands
Brushes his hair
Brushes his teeth

She will always have him with her
Something that sounds nice
But for tougher reasons
It is not

Typical

The autumn returns
Predictably
But without cynicism
The giant ash
miraculous
for a week
And then
Seemed paltry
In comparison to the
Smaller cherry tree
Two-coloured
Bright red
And a sort of pink
And orange
Typical in everyway
Sitting in front of the 1960's house
Nothing special
A frontage road
An old pickup truck
Blocking the low sun
Children walking right past
Noticing nothing
As if the miracle
Might happen again

Voicemail

Dada, did you get the message?

He stutters a bit
And then goes back to phrasing:
I love you and I miss you.

Milo is being nice to me now
We are going on a school bus
It's my birthday soon
I can't wait to go to Florida.

And then he is prompted by his mother.

I can't wait for guy's weekend
I got a new robot
I got a book about dinosaurs
I fed Alfie
She is on the bed with us.

I love you and I miss you
Banana.

So much softer than I did back then

Three
       or four
Long lines
       in the sky
Brightened by
       a setting sun
Moving to pink
       from white.

They force us
       to stop
Turn our heads
       sideways
             the way collies do.
The city walkers
       Stop
             bumping into each other

In looking up,
       they try
             to find something poignant
In thoughts
       now completely diffuse
             unattainable, and
                   unimportant

Acknowledgments

This book includes 42 previously published poems. I very much appreciate all the editors from these literary journals for accepting my work. They are: Water on land. 2013. *Innisfree Poetry Journal*; Children. 2013. *Angle Journal of Poetry*; Light. 2013. *Poetry Pacific*; The seaside. 2013. *Exercise Bowler*; Then time. 2013. *Dead Flowers*; Evening. 2014. *Poetry Quarterly*; He says. 2014. *Poetry Quarterly*; Photographs. 2014. *Poetry Quarterly*; War. 2014. *Three and a half point 9*; Morning. 2014. *Poetry Quarterly*; Barely talking. 2014. *Poetry Quarterly*; Harbinger. 2014. *Literary Juice*; Birds. 2014. *Garbanzo Literary Journal*; Chords. 2014. *Garbanzo Literary Journal*; Shared. 2014. *Vox Poetica*; Conjuring. 2014. *Vox Poetica*; Puddles. 2014. *BlazeVox*; Coda. 2014. *BlazeVox*; Acquisition. 2014. *BlazeVox*; Equations. 2015. *Indefinite Space*; Love Goes Downhill. 2015. *The Write Place. BlazeVox*; Peat. 2015. *The Write Place. BlazeVox*; My little boy asks. 2015. *Works and Days Quarterly*; Arriving. 2015. *Bitchin' Kitch*; Window. 2015. *Eunoia Review*; My little boy is sitting on flowers. 2015. *Drunk Monkeys*; Sunrise. 2015. *Drunk Monkeys*; Next to me. 2015. *Blotterature*; The plane. 2015. Fiction Week Literary Review; Faith. 2015. *Corner Club Press*; Hurry and wait. 2016. *Corner Club Press*; Skype. 2015. *Forge Journal*; Typical. 2015. *Danse Macabre*; Bedtime. 2015. *Former people*; Flies. 2016. *Mandala Journal*; So much softer than I did back then. 2016. *The Opiate*; Breathing (new name). 2016. *Los Angeles Review of Los Angeles*; Commuting. 2016. *Inwood Indiana Press*; Voicemail. 2016. *Packingtown Review*; Liver. 2016. *Packingtown Review*; Screens. 2016. *FishFood Magazine*; Dublin. 2019. *Blue Lake Review*

Morgan has published more than 100 poems and six short stories in literary journals. He is also a well-published essayist. He is a professor of thermodynamics with a focus on the Second Law, and a semi-professional ski racer and fly fisherman. In the storm years of his strength, he was a professional mountain guide in the Himalaya. As a boy, he was in a well-known jazz fusion quartet known as "The Bermuda Rectangle". He lives with his family and dog, Potato, in the hills of Colorado.

www.ingramcontent.com/pod-product-compliance
Lightning Source LLC
Chambersburg PA
CBHW030059170426
43197CB00010B/1586